YOUNG PEOPLE AND CRIME

THE DONALD WINNICOTT MEMORIAL LECTURE

YOUNG PEOPLE AND CRIME
Improving Provision for Children Who Offend

Given by

Professor Rod Morgan

and

Professor Sheila Hollins

Appendix

Winnicott's Contribution to

the Study of Dangerousness

Brett Kahr

Published by
KARNAC
on behalf of
THE WINNICOTT CLINIC OF PSYCHOTHERAPY
Registered Charity No. 260427
London, 2004

Published in 2006 by
Karnac (Books) Ltd.
6 Pembroke Buildings, London NW10 6RE
on behalf of
The Winnicott Clinic of Psychotherapy
PO Box 233
Ruislip
Middlesex HA4 8UJ

British Library Cataloguing in Publication Data

A C.I.P. for this book is available from the British Library

ISBN 1 85575 460 6

Edited, designed, and produced by The Studio Publishing Services Ltd,
www.publishingservicesuk.co.uk
E-mail: studio@publishingservicesuk.co.uk

Printed in Great Britain

www.karnacbooks.com

CONTENTS

Sheila Hollins taught science in Nigeria as a volunteer before studying medicine at St Thomas's. After three years in general practice she trained in psychiatry, retaining a strong interest in people's physical health. This is reflected in her research interests, which include health inequalities, end of life care, clinical outcomes following bereavement, and abuse in psychiatry of learning disabilities. During her career she has had a broad influence across many fields of psychiatry, especially in learning disability, child psychiatry, psychotherapy, and trauma. She has worked at the Department of Health, London, as a senior policy adviser, and been a member of the Learning Disability Taskforce. Professor Hollins is the current President of the Royal College of Psychiatrists.

Brett Kahr is Senior Lecturer in Psychotherapy in the School of Psychotherapy and Counselling at Regent's College in London, as well as a psychotherapist and marital psychotherapist in private practice. In 2001, the Winnicott Clinic of Psychotherapy appointed him as the first Winnicott Clinic Senior Research fellow in Psychotherapy. He is a Patron of The Squiggle Foundation, and a Trustee of the Institute of Psychotherapy and Disability, as well as the Special Media Adviser to The United Kingdom Council for Psychotherapy, and Consultant at the Centre for Attachment-Based Psychoanalytic Psychotherapy. His books include *D. W. Winnicott: A Biographical Portrait*, which won the Gradiva Award for Biography in 1997, as well as *Forensic Psychotherapy and Psychopathology: Winnicottian Perspectives*, and *The Legacy of Winnicott: Essays on Infant and Child Mental Health*, all published by Karnac.

Eric Koops, LVO, is the Chairman of the Trustees of the Winnicott Clinic of Psychotherapy, the registered charity responsible for the annual Donald Winnicott Memorial Lecture.

The Clinic was founded in 1969 to promote professional training in the principles of psychotherapy, to conduct research, and to assist in the provision of individual psychotherapy. During the 1990s, to meet changing circumstances, assistance was extended to patients in group therapy, training grants were awarded, and symposia arranged to encourage organizations to reduce workplace stress. Since 2000, the main focus of Clinic activities has been the wider dissemination of the work and ideas of Dr Donald W. Winnicott (1896–1971), the distinguished English paediatrician, child psychiatrist and psychoanalyst, who made an outstanding contribution to an understanding of the causes of mental illness, particularly in infants and children. To this end, the Clinic established the Winnicott Clinic Senior Research Fellowship in Psychotherapy and Counselling, and the annual Donald Winnicott Memorial Lecture, designed for a wide audience of professionals and others involved with children. Lectures focus upon specific topics arising from Winnicott's life and ideas, in terms of relevance for twenty-first century living.

Rod Morgan is Chairman of the Youth Justice Board, a post he has held since April 2004. Prior to that he was HM Chief Inspector of Probation for England and Wales and before that Professor of Criminal Justice in the Faculty of Law, University of Bristol, where he remains Professor Emeritus. He is the author of many books and articles on aspects of criminal justice, ranging from policing to sentencing. He is a specialist adviser to Amnesty International and the Council of Europe on custodial conditions and torture, a topic on which he has written extensively, including the Council of Europe's official guide to the European Convention for the Prevention of Torture. He is also co-editor of *The Oxford Handbook of Criminology* (OUP, fourth edition, in press) and is currently preparing a handbook on probation policy, research and practice (Willan, forthcoming). He sits on several advisory committees for voluntary organizations working in the field of youth and criminal justice and, during his career, he has held practically every lay office (magistrate, police authority member, Parole Board member, etc.) that it is possible to hold within the criminal justice field.

Foreword

Young people and crime

Eric Koops

I t gives me great pleasure to welcome you here tonight to this, the Fourth Donald Winnicott Memorial Lecture arranged by the Winnicott Clinic of Psychotherapy. We have held each Lecture in one of the King's College buildings and tonight we are using a new hall where chairs have those little fold-down tables that may be useful for taking notes.

Let me begin by saying a little about the Clinic. It is a registered charity and is therefore governed by Trustees—Leo Abse, Lord Jones, Christine Miqueu-Baz, Cesare Sacerdoti, with myself as Chairman; some of you may have met us at previous Lectures. We all come from very different backgrounds and have a wide range of experience, bringing approaches of a diverse nature to the way we operate. We are a not a large charity but, to paraphrase Professor Schumacher's famous declaration in 1973: "Small can be Beautiful". One advantage of our size is that Trustees can take decisions fairly speedily; we are fortunate to have a small capital fund, the income from which basically covers administration costs.

We were founded in 1969, originally to encourage professional training in psychotherapy, to conduct research, and assist individuals of limited means able to benefit from psychotherapy. During the

1

thirty-five years of our existence we have had a wide range of activities; those of an educational nature are now at the fore. Since 2000, we have concentrated on the wider dissemination of the work and ideas of Dr Donald Woods Winnicott, the distinguished English paediatrician, child psychiatrist, and psychoanalyst who made such an outstanding contribution to the understanding of the causes of mental illness, particularly those relating to infants and children. We set up a research fellowship and instituted this annual Memorial Lecture. Lectures have focused on a variety of topics, tackled by various speakers, which have attracted diverse audiences—ranging from people working with disturbed children and adolescents, many students and academics involved in psychotherapy, and also a fair proportion of people working with the young in everyday situations: in nurseries, playgroups, schools, and youth clubs.

Our inaugural speaker in 2002 was Dr Joyce McDougall, a long-standing colleague and friend of Donald Winnicott, who reflected upon Winnicott both personally and as the analyst inspiring her own psychoanalytic career. She began her training at the Hampstead Institute in the early 1950s; Joyce was with Anna Freud at one stage in her career herself—an extraordinary link with the past. In 2003 we were privileged to have Sir Richard Bowlby surveying "Fifty Years of Attachment Theory", pioneered by his father Dr John Bowlby. That concept, of emotional development being affected by the relationship between infants and their main carer, is much less controversial today. On that occasion Pearl King, who I am pleased to see is with us here tonight, and who is one of the few people alive today who worked with both John Bowlby and Donald Winnicott in a variety of contexts, also shared recollections of these two pioneering figures of British psychoanalysis. Professor André Green was with us last year and it was a very different lecture to what we had anticipated. He surprised us all by focusing on points in psychoanalytic theory where their ideas differed. The printed version of his paper was expanded to include some very interesting conjectures about the relationships between Wynne Godley, Masud Khan, and Donald Winnicott.

We are fortunate to have developed a very good relationship with Karnac Books over these Lectures, and they have published each one on our behalf. I hope you all had a chance to look at

Karnac's selection this evening—they included some of Professor Hollins's books; those of you who have not managed to see them, please contact our Trust Secretary, Frances Hawkins, who will be able to assist.

And so we come to the Memorial Lecture of 2005. The topic, "Young people and crime", arose as a direct result of feedback from previous audiences. Sadly, it is a subject whose importance has increased greatly over the past decade or so. Young people are today perceived as becoming more and more aggressive, privately and in public, as individuals and in groups; they are sometimes the victims of crime and aggression as well being the perpetrators. We have two speakers to tackle the subject this evening: Professor Rod Morgan, here in his capacity as Chairman of the Youth Justice Board; and Professor Sheila Hollins, Head of the Academic Division of Mental Health at St George's, University of London.

Professor Rod Morgan made life easier for those who did not know him when, in his capacity as Chairman of the Youth Justice Board, he wrote to *The Times* in September 2004. This was in response to an article by Libby Purves pointing out the daily dilemma faced by the Board of balancing the requirements of the courts with the need to ensure that once young people are in custody, they are subject to constructive regimes. He wrote: "There are still too many children in custody. We have developed community-based alternatives"—but there are not enough to meet the need; one of the Board's aims is to make the work of the Prison Service more "child-centred" and it welcomes opportunities that help provide a better-informed public debate. Rod has had a very interesting academic career in this field, and a practising one. He was, for example a lay magistrate for over twenty years and is no stranger in the youth courts or remand centres, or to the police authority or the parole boards, and has served on numerous working parties and committees concerned with criminal justice. In the more academic area, aspects of policing and penal policy have come within his ambit and he is a recognized Expert Adviser on custodial conditions to the Council of Europe and to Amnesty International. After being a Professor of Criminal Justice in the Faculty of Law at Bristol University for some years, he has remained there as Professor Emeritus.

Clearly two of the more pressing problems for the Youth Justice Board is the sheer number of young people in custody and how few alternative regimes are available. Crime and young people, children in custody, are two very emotive issues; they are also extraordinarily complex. We are very lucky to have Rod Morgan with us to help us understand them better.

Ladies and Gentlemen, Professor Rod Morgan.

Improving provision for children who offend

Rod Morgan

Setting the scene

The Youth Justice Board (YJB), which I have the honour to chair, does not provide services. It commissions and purchases them. And monitors contract compliance and general performance by those agencies that do deliver youth justice services. The latter include the 155 local authority youth offending teams (YOTs) in England and Wales and the various agencies—the Prison Service, several commercial companies and a number of local authorities—that provide closed residential accommodation for those children and young persons, or juveniles, who the criminal courts determine must be held in custody (for a general overview of the role of the YJB see YJB 2004a).

There are currently approximately 2800 children and young persons, aged 10–17 years inclusive, in custody. Most older children aged 15–17—and with this audience, as when I talk to sentencers, I am going to refer to them as children so as to emphasize their status in law and our international rights obligations to them—are overwhelmingly accommodated in Prison Service-managed Young Offender Institutions (YOIs). Those of middling years, and older children who, for one reason or another, cannot cope with life on the mainstream in YOIs, are generally held in one of four commercially-operated Secure Training Centres (STCs). And younger children are generally held in the fifteen local authority secure community homes (LASCHs) with which the YJB contracts.

The YJB has been responsible for commissioning and purchasing custodial provision for juveniles since 2000. We have made considerable progress in improving the quality of what is provided. Healthcare and educational programmes and facilities have greatly improved. Staff are better trained. Considerable investment has been made in accommodation and other buildings. These improvements have been attested in successive reports from the various inspectorates (Commission for Social Care Inspection (CSCI) and HMI Prisons) who regularly scrutinize what is provided. Yet we are the first to acknowledge that there is a considerable way to go.

Our capacity to make progress is determined by two principal factors—the budget allocated to us by the Home Office, and the sentencing trend. I doubt the first will be increased in the next year or so. Thus, our principal efforts are directed towards the second factor. We are committed to persuading sentencers that they can confidently resort less to custody, at both the remand and sentencing stage. We believe that most serious and persistent child offenders can be more effectively, humanely, and cheaply dealt with by means of community-based measures. To this end the YJB has developed some robust arrangements that go by the name of Intensive Supervision and Surveillance Programmes (ISSP), in which electronic surveillance and/or tracking is combined with intensive engagement with the young offenders for at least twenty-five hours a week. There will, of course, always be some children who have to be kept in custody, and you may ask me how many fewer children I think should be in custody. I can't and won't put a figure on it. Let us simply say: substantially fewer.

At the end of 2003 it seemed that we were having some success with the courts in this regard. The number of children in custody had, in the previous fifteen months, declined by about twelve per cent. However, in the first four months of 2004 there was a disturbing reversal, and although during the rest of the year the custodial population more or less flat-lined, by the end of 2004 we had lost much of the ground that we thought we had made. So far this year we are holding steady. But I remain anxious and am far from complacent.

What do these population pressures mean? We aim to have 8–10% headroom between population and custodial beds available. We need that headroom. The available places are never entirely in the right place at the right time. Nor are they always suitable for the individual offenders we have to allocate to them. But over the past year we have consistently had much less than the desirable headroom. We have occasionally been close to having a full house. When this happens things are much more likely to go wrong. Children are more likely to have to be placed further from home. We are less likely to be able to find a suitable place. The result is stress for everyone concerned. Above all for the children, but also for their parents or carers and, of course, for the staff who have to deal with the resultant tensions. When the system is overcrowded serious incidents are more likely to occur—incidents of self-harm, of vandalism, of strife. You will be aware that during the past year, in the period that I have been YJB Chairman, there have been three deaths of children or young persons in custody, two by suicide and one while being restrained.

We deal with some of the most troubled and troublesome children in our society. Their problems are typically multi-faceted. They are often from families that have repeatedly broken down. The children have generally been ill-served by mainstream services. They are typically drawn from the most deprived neighbourhoods. Quite often they have been excluded from school, officially or unofficially, or their non-attendance has been colluded with by the educational services, for prolonged periods. They have generally had poor health care. They are often abusers of alcohol and illicit drugs. They have frequently been engaged in sexual activity from an early age. I like to sum the situation up by saying that they often have a street age of thirty, a chronological age of fifteen, and a literacy and numeracy age of eight. This is not an easy mix.

In what follows I want to do three things. First, to paint an epidemiological sketch of the mental and developmental characteristics of our population. Second, by way of illustration, to provide one or two case study examples of our more acute problems. Third, I want to describe the strategy we are adopting to address these problems.

I should emphasize that I have no expertise in the mental health or psychology fields and I know relatively little about the work of Donald Winnicott, the psychotherapy pioneer whose memory this lecture honours. I apologize for that and will look to Sheila Hollins to fill the gap. I merely report some research and clinical findings. But I know one thing about Donald Winnicott's work. That is, he emphasized that the gaining of trust was key to healthy human mental development.

My concern is for the safety and well-being of children who are drawn into the youth justice system for which I am responsible. My experience of meeting the too many children that in England and Wales the courts commit to custody is that human trust is the characteristic that typically they lack. This is scarcely surprising. For typically they have repeatedly been failed by the adults—those in their families and the public services with whom they have contact. They have been kicked, often literally, from pillar to post, shunted into desolate corners, cast off. To work effectively with this group of children, time is desperately short. They are rapidly approaching adulthood. Perceived family and statutory responsibilities for them evaporate rapidly as they approach the age of eighteen. No one particularly wants them or wishes to take responsibility for them. They are unattractive trouble. As they approach adulthood they are increasingly regarded as undeserving. Punishment, not help; control, not support; contempt, not respect, is more and more their lot.

My overriding concern is that these children should have access to the mainstream services they need and which, typically, have failed them, and that they should gain positive experience from which trust might develop. For to the extent that we fail in this regard, these children are likely to become the adults with whom we will come to be in a state of civil war—at great cost to our humanity, our public tranquillity, and our public expenditure budget.

The mental health profile of our population

All children receiving a Final Warning from the police or brought before the criminal courts for an offence should be assessed by YOT workers using a more-or-less comprehensive assessment tool termed ASSET. It is not universally done and the assessment tool is not always used well or to the full. Nevertheless, according to aggregate ASSET-derived data, and the additional mental health and drug use screening tools we employ, 15% of YOT-assessed children are said to have mental health problems (for overview, see YJB, 2001). However, more focused epidemiological studies (for example, Harrington and Bailey, forthcoming) of young offenders under supervision or in custody reveal the following more demanding picture:

- 31% have mental health needs;
- 18% have problems with depression;
- 10% suffer from anxiety;
- 9% report a history of self-harm in the preceding month;
- 9% suffer from PTSD;
- 7% are characterized by hyperactivity;
- 5% report psychotic-like symptoms.

A very high proportion have learning difficulties. That is:

- 23% have a measured IQ of 69 or below;
- an additional 36% have borderline learning difficulties—IQs in the range 70–79;
- fewer than 3% have IQs of 110+.

The overwhelming majority (83%) have a reading age and reading comprehension age (92%) below their chronological age. Whereas the surveyed children have a mean chronological age of sixteen years, their mean reading age is 11.3 years and their reading comprehension age is ten years.

These findings are scarcely surprising given the typically low levels of education engagement. Three quarters of these young people have a history of school exclusion or expulsion and general attendance levels are typically poor. It is common among those of school age in custody for them not to have attended school for months or years.

Offending is, of course, a principal factor in these careers of social marginalization. Whereas a little over half have committed ten or fewer offences, a sizeable minority—approximately one fifth—are prolific offenders with fifty or more offences to their name. Further, among all children dealt with by the youth justice system substance misuse is high. Among those in custody, one study suggests that:

- 40% have been dependent on a substance at some point in their lives;
- 74% report having drunk alcohol more than once a week with the majority of the drinkers regularly exceeding six units on a single drinking occasion;
- 83% are regular smokers;
- what I will describe as "self-medication" is common—30% report that they have taken drugs not to get high but just to "feel normal" and 38% say they have taken a drug to "forget everything" or "blot everything out".

"Risky" behaviour with regard to use of alcohol and illicit drugs is often combined with precociously risky sexual activity and troubled family relationships.

The YJB, in partnership with the Home Office, the DfES and the DoH, has been prioritizing the improvement of YOT partnership working with the Child and Adolescent Mental Health Services (CAMHS) and enhancing provision within the closed estate. But provision across the country is patchy and we still have significant problems.

Since I became Chair of the YJB in April 2004, two events have given sharp focus to the mental health problems we face.

Case studies

Last August, 2004, a fifteen-year-old youth, Adam Rickwood, hanged himself at Hassockfield STC. It was the first suicide in an STC. Three weeks ago, in January 2005, another child, Gareth Price, aged sixteen, hanged himself at Lancaster Farms YOI. I cannot speak further about these cases because the investigations are ongoing and their outcomes are not yet known. But I can speak about another case.

Within three weeks of my taking up office the inquest took place into the death of Joseph Scholes, who hanged himself at Stoke Heath YOI in March 2002. In order to prepare myself for the publicity I knew would result, I went to Stoke Heath in my second week.

Joseph was nine days into a two-year Detention and Training Order (DTO) imposed by Manchester Crown Court for offences of robbery involving theft of mobile phones, committed with other children with whom Joseph had absconded from a residential home where he was subject to a Police Protection Order. He was in temporary care partly because of a history of violence against his mother. He had been diagnosed as having a depressive conduct disorder, exacerbated by his abuse of alcohol and other substances. He had a history of self-harm. He was initially allocated to Stoke Heath by the YJB placements team because, on the day in question, there was no place for him in a LASCH. Because of his history of vulnerability and self-harm he was accommodated in the Stoke Heath health care centre.

Stoke Heath is a grim, split-site establishment, accommodating juveniles in one section and young adult prisoners in another. I knew from HMI Prison reports that Stoke Heath had greatly improved since Joseph Scholes died and I was impressed by the senior management with whom I met. They acknowledged the shortcomings in their buildings, other facilities, and the regime, but convinced me that things were improving and that they wanted to make things better. But they were constrained locally as the YJB is constrained nationally: we both have to employ the infrastructure we have inherited.

Before I went to the health centre where Joseph Scholes died, the governor told me it was "not fit for purpose". When I saw the health centre, which I am glad to report has since closed and been replaced with a new, purpose-built centre, I could not but agree with him.

I saw the room where Joseph Scholes hanged himself. It was miserable—almost designed to intensify the cloud of despair under which he was labouring. What disturbed me most, however, was that in an adjacent, identical room was another young man. I asked that I be allowed to enter his room and talk to him. I entered. But I could not really have a conversation with him. He was uncommunicative, monosyllabic, seemed very depressed. Afterwards, I asked to see his file. I concluded that he had very similar symptoms to Joseph Scholes. Let me share with you some details regarding this sixteen-year-old youth—who I shall call John (not his real name) so that you will appreciate what I mean.

In September 2003 John was remanded in custody by the Crown Court, awaiting trial for arson of a dwelling. He was judged highly vulnerable by the YOT worker who assessed him because:

- his offence involved setting fire to his own flat in order to take his own life;
- he had a history of self-harm;
- he had a history of being bullied and teased, of being treated like a "village idiot";
- he had previously been on the Child Protection Register;
- he displayed depression-like symptoms;
- he had learning and emotional difficulties;
- he was an alcohol and illegal drug user.

We placed him at one of the four STCs. And during the three months before he was eventually sentenced he stayed there. The court sentenced him to two-and-a-half years' custody.

The STC thought it inappropriate that he stay with them on sentence. It was felt that he was not mentally ill. But he self-harmed. Thus, in January 2004 he was transferred to Stoke Heath, the YOI closest to John's home in Cheshire.

Very soon after his transfer John's response was giving the YJB monitor cause for concern. The Stoke Heath authorities felt he had to be accommodated in their health unit due to his persistent self-harm attempts. He made a very serious suicide attempt resulting in the staff having to cut down a ligature. He repeatedly threw himself wildly at the walls. He was being medicated and the Stoke Heath GP was trying to get him psychiatrically assessed with a view to sectioning him. It had so far been to no avail but John's behaviour was so life-threatening that we, the YJB, provided Stoke Heath with additional funding so that dedicated staff could spend additional time with him.

A case conference in May brought all parties together to discuss the situation. John was being permanently sedated and his physical health was deteriorating. Psychiatrists from the Gardner Unit in

Manchester were now to assess him, but psychiatric opinions so far obtained did not accept that John was hearing the voices he claimed to be hearing or that he was mentally ill. John was reluctant to accept visits from his mother and though she said she would have him home on release she did not believe she could cope with him if his present condition continued.

In May assessments from three different psychiatrists were sought but the Cheshire PCT were reluctant to offer funding. One of the doctors, a Child and Adolescent Psychiatrist, did not feel that John had a schizophrenic-type illness. Eventually, in October 2004, eleven months after the start of his sentence and with his necessary release becoming imminent, John was sectioned under the Mental Health Act and transferred to the Ardenleigh Clinic. Throughout the summer his self-harming attempts continued, as did our special funding arrangements to provide additional care in a YOI totally ill-equipped to cater for John's condition.

John's case is not exceptional. I visited an STC very recently and was told of another sixteen-year-old youth who the establishment had received following sentence—in his case, eighteen months. This youth's behaviour was so disturbed that the accommodation unit in which he was held could be used only partially. All attempts to get the young man sectioned during the nine months before he *had* to be released failed. In the event he was sectioned at the gate on the day he was released. I think the inference is clear. If our providers of penal custody can in some sense cope, they may be made by the health authorities to cope until the day comes when the risk and responsibility is irrevocably that of the health authorities.

We recently organized a day-long seminar for 40–50 Crown Court judges who regularly deal with juveniles. The issue that preoccupied them the most was what to do with young offenders whose cases have repeatedly to be adjourned and who are remanded in custody awaiting psychiatric reports on the grounds that all the available evidence suggests, at least to relatively lay observers, that they are mentally ill. Frequently, the judges told us, they felt they could adjourn no longer and sentenced these youths to a lengthy period in custody for want of any apparent alternative.

I cannot say that this was the view of the judge in the case of Joseph Scholes. However, we do know the results of the Scholes inquest, which was conducted with a jury, and we know the outcome of various other investigations into that death, with a further investigation, being conducted on behalf of the Home Secretary, yet to be completed. There is so far general agreement as follows:

- that Joseph's custodial sentence was inappropriate;
- that he was inappropriately placed in a YOI, albeit there were difficulties making available a LASCH place, which would have been the best;
- the quality of the ASSET was deficient—it should have spelt out in greater evidential detail why he was considered so vulnerable;
- there was poor communication between the relevant parties— the fact, for example, that Joseph's YOT worker specifically requested, following his initial placement, that he be transferred to a LASCH was not made known to the YOI, who thought he was settling in and failed to pick up certain danger signs in his behaviour;
- the health care centre at Stoke Heath was unfit for its purpose.

Next steps

What are we, the YJB, doing to address this unsatisfactory situation?

Our major tasks are to educate all the key stakeholders in the field as to the dilemmas we face and persuade the courts that there are community-based alternatives in which they can have confidence so as to reduce the pressures on the custodial population as a whole, thereby enabling us to do a better job for the children who must continue to be in our custodial care. To this end we issued a consultative document in the late autumn regarding the secure estate for juveniles (YJB, 2004b). This document sets out our current thinking. It is a mixture of principles and pragmatism. It states our objectives and describes what we think we can feasibly do within the next three years.

Let me highlight certain features of our thinking:

- First, we have to work closely with all our providers. That means establishing longer-term trusting partnerships with them. There are no local authorities queuing up to provide LASCHs, nor is there a queue of private contractors wishing to enter the field. We have to plan *with* our providers. That means sharing our thinking with them and entering into longer-term agreements with them: we can't expect them to invest in buildings, regimes, staff training, etc., if they have no confidence that we will continue to use them. Thus, we have moved from a one- to a three-year service level agreement with the Prison Service. That is also why we have said that we do not, in the foreseeable future, plan to reduce the number of LASCH and STC beds we purchase.

- Second, we aim to develop several smaller, more intensively staffed, more child-centred "support" or "intermediate" (in the sense that they will be more like the LASCHs and STCs) units for the 200–300 older children (15–17-year-olds) who, for one reason or another, cannot cope with mainstream life in the YOIs. We are surveying the estate with a view to identifying suitable locations. If we cannot, in the short term, greatly increase the number of children *not* accommodated outside the Prison Service estate, then we must do a better job inside it to protect particularly vulnerable children.

- Third, we must press for an inter-departmental strategy, involving the Home Office, the DfES, and the DoH, to plan for secure and semi-secure provision for three classes of children who, in a number of respects, are not so distinct: children proceeded against in the criminal courts; children who, as a result of civil proceedings, are in the care of the local authorities; and children who are mentally ill and/or have learning disabilities. These groups are not so distinct because: the research evidence indicates that criminalized and cared-for children often have very similar characteristics; it is something of a lottery as to whether troubled and troublesome children are dealt with by means of civil or criminal proceedings; and, as we have seen, the agencies who provide the accommodation for the three groups trade on each other's goodwill or services.

Thus, to amplify the last point:

- Cared-for children whose behaviour in residential settings is especially difficult are all too easily criminalized.

- Criminalized children in custody have very often also been subject to care orders—the LASCHs provide for both groups.
- Criminalized children, as we have seen, often have profound mental health difficulties and, because of the paucity of secure or semi-secure beds for juveniles in the mental health sector— there are currently forty-eight NHS beds (ten in Manchester, eighteen in Newcastle, and twenty in Birmingham) and there are forty further beds (two x ten in London and twenty in Southampton) due to open by 2007 plus eighty voluntary/ private beds at Northampton.
- The health services often tend, understandably, to stand off from their responsibilities while those children are in penal custody.
- The PCTs and local authorities are very reluctant to provide the very expensive beds about which we are talking unless they are given a guarantee that those beds will be purchased long-term and remain full—a requirement that an agency like the YJB cannot easily fulfil.

These dilemmas are not easily resolved, not least because of the perverse financial incentives that operate. If a child is taken into care, the cost falls on the local authority. If the child is criminalized and remanded or sentenced to custody, the YJB pays centrally. Which is why we must adopt strategies that are a mixture of principle and pragmatism. The starting point should always be the paramount interests of the child and the five outcome tests that the Children Act 2004 has established. Thereafter, responsibilities need to be allocated and funding provided so as effectively to limit the likelihood that decisions will be made in individual cases that fail to protect and that enhance the likelihood that positive treatment will be delivered. For me, this challenge is among my highest priorities.

References

DfES (2003). *Every Child Matters*. London: DfES.
Harrington, R., & Bailey, S. (forthcoming). *The Mental Health Needs and Effectiveness of Provision for Young Offenders in Custody and in the Community*. London: Youth Justice Board.

YJB (2001). *Risk and protective factors associated with youth crime amd effective interventions to prevent it*, London: Youth Justice Board.

YJB (2004a). *Building in Confidence: Annual Review 2003–4*. London: Youth Justice Board.

YJB (2004b). *Consultative Paper on Strategy for the Secure Estate*. London: Youth Justice Board.

Introduction of
Sheila Hollins

Eric Koops

T hank you very much, Rod. There were two points from your
talk that struck me as particularly important for us all to
remember: first the sad, "No one wants them" and, leading
on from that, the reminder that our failure with these children
results in disaster in both financial and human terms.

That leads us to our second guest this evening, Professor Sheila
Hollins. I must begin by congratulating her, on behalf of all of us
here, on her recent election as President of the Royal College of
Psychiatrists, a College that has been in existence in some form or
another since 1841, and I believe she is only the second female to
hold this office in the history of the College. Many congratulations
and good wishes.

There was a little piece of Winnicottian influence very early in
Sheila's career, for she was a House Surgeon at Paddington Green
Children's Hospital in London, where Donald Winnicott worked as
physician, and then consultant, for some forty years. Today, she is
based at St George's Medical School, a College of the University of
London, in St George's Hospital, Tooting. This is a specialized
College of Medicine and Health Science, independently governed
and funded, with a particularly strong research base. Sheila is its

Professor of Psychiatry of Learning Disability, and Head of its Academic Department of Mental Health.

Sheila's career shows a growing interest and expertise in the field of learning disabilities. She served on the Advisory Group, set up in the wake of the Mansell Report, on "Challenging Behaviour and Mental Health Needs", and was twice seconded to the Department of Health as Senior Policy Adviser on Learning Disability and Autism. In addition to numerous publications on intellectual disability and mental health, Sheila is editor of *Books Beyond Words*, the prize-winning series of counselling picture-books on health topics for people unable to read. Quite often such people, when still at school, are regarded as failures because they inevitably fall behind the rest of the class, and are too often written off because their behaviour, arising from frustration when attempts to learn fail, can become disruptive and aggressive. Very slowly, we are beginning to understand that the under-achievement that leads to aggression could well be the result of developmental disorders which have failed to be identified, either early enough or at all. I would suggest that it is the early recognition of these disorders, and early appropriate interventions, that are most likely to prevent such children ending up in trouble at home, at school, in the community and, ultimately, being brought before the Magistrates as "young offenders".

Ladies and Gentlemen, Professor Sheila Hollins.

Young people with learning disabilities and challenging behaviour: a Winnicottian perspective

Sheila Hollins

I first heard of Donald Winnicott when I was a house surgeon at Paddington Green Children's Hospital in 1970, where his work was still very much revered. It is a real honour to be invited to co-present the Fourth Donald Winnicott Memorial Lecture—and the invitation encouraged me to recall the ways in which Winnicott's work and writings may have influenced my thinking.

I would, however, like to begin by commenting on something Professor Morgan said; he said he "didn't know anything about mental health"—yet it seemed to me that his talk did in fact show enormous understanding and compassion for the mental health and the emotional needs of the young people for whom he is commissioning services. There is this interesting puzzle: the idea that somehow emotional distress is disconnected from mental health. That has always seemed to me to be somewhat anomalous. I have at times been told that my own work and interests are more about emotion than mental illness or mental health, but I do not see that there is such a huge difference between them.

I had always intended to be a paediatrician, but working 108 hours a week in a training post, which was the norm then, was just not compatible when I also had a small child. I went into general practice instead, which certainly did seem a more manageable career at that stage. After three years as a GP in South London, I realized that I knew insufficient about both the emotional and social lives of my patients to be able to attend to the complex inter-relationships between their health and well-being, and also environmental and other factors in their lives. I began psychiatric training with the intention of returning to general practice. I had an excellent training in psychiatry, partly because I was able to train part-time. I started just when part-time training for women was introduced into medicine, and it meant I had a lot of choice about the precise placements that I could have and, of course, each rotation was longer than usual and that was advantageous. I was very lucky to have Dr A. Brafman and Dr M. Micholopoulos as consultants at this early stage of my psychiatric training, both of whom are also psychoanalysts. I decided to train as a child and adolescent psychiatrist because I thought it would enable me to bring together my growing interest in psychotherapy with work with families and children. I enjoyed two years at the Earls Court Child Guidance Unit, where my psychotherapeutic work was mainly supervised by Renata Putzel.

Until then I had had no clinical exposure at all to learning disabilities. However, my second child, a son, was becoming recognized as having learning difficulties and, perhaps in response to my growing insights into the issues faced by such children, I found that my case-load increasingly included children who were disabled or different in some way. In 1980 I went to talk to Joan Bicknell, who had just been appointed the first Professor of the Psychiatry of Mental Handicap in the United Kingdom; that term, "Mental Handicap" has since been changed to Learning or Intellectual Disability. She recruited me to a Senior Lecturer post—with some difficulty, I might add, but she was very persuasive. The result is that for twenty-five years now (in 2005) a group at St George's in Tooting has been involved in service development, professional training, and research, always with the aim of making a difference to the mental and emotional health of people with learning disabilities. Our focus was increasingly upon adults rather than children. When I was appointed, Professor Bicknell was very proud to announce that she had recruited a psychotherapist, because she recognized the potential contribution that psychotherapy could make to our work with people with learning disabilities, and because she was a psychotherapist herself.

In a radio talk for parents that Winnicott gave in 1946, the year of my birth incidentally, he was asked the question, "What do we mean by a normal child?"—I haven't asked my mother whether she listened to this series of talks. Winnicott explained that life is normally difficult for any child, but he ended the lecture with a friendly hint; he said, "Put a lot of store in a child's ability to play. If a child is playing, there is room for a symptom or two. If a child is able to enjoy play . . . there is no very serious trouble afoot" (Winnicott, 1946). Later on he wrote that "psychotherapy has to do with two people playing together" (Winnicott, 1965). The corollary of this is that where playing is not possible, then the work done by the therapist is directed towards bringing the patient from a state of not being able to play into a state of being able to play.

I had what one might call a Winnicottian experience a couple of weeks ago on a train journey. It was the weekend when I had intended to start work on this talk. I settled down on the train with my reading, and with paper and pencil—and then realized I was not going to get any work done at all because facing me was a little girl who was very active. She was jumping up and down; she was crawling on the floor; she was basically being very busy. It was clear that they were going almost the same distance as me. She was called Amy and was with what seemed like her teenage Mum, going to visit her Dad with a small birthday cake. Mum had a puzzle-book for herself but had nothing for the child. Amy took the puzzle-book and at that stage I decided I should play with her. She rolled the puzzle-book up and looked at me; we were playing a game of whether she could tell what colour my eyes were when looking through the tube. After a while I suggested she might like to draw a picture for me and I gave her my pencil and pad. She drew a picture of Little Red Riding-Hood; not a very mature picture for a girl who was four years old, but it was a nice picture and when I commented on it she said, "I'm going to draw a sister for Little Red Riding-Hood." The sister was a much bigger version of Little Red Riding-Hood and I said, "Has she got a name?" Amy could not think of one. I said, "What about Big Red Riding-Hood? Or is she Little Blue Riding-Hood? What shall we call her?" Amy thought all this was very amusing, and then rubbed out both of the pictures—

at which point Mother announced that it was time to go. They disappeared and the man sitting next to me said: "You were wonderful! What do you do?" When I just smiled, he said, "Are you a teacher?" I said, "No. Actually, I'm a psychiatrist." And that was the end of our conversation!

While I was thinking about what I would say tonight, I have been really enjoying re-reading some of Donald Winnicott's writings but, perhaps unsurprisingly, I could find very little in Winnicott's writings about children with learning disabilities— although they very often have difficulty in learning to play. That is why I think his insights have relevance for therapy with children with learning disabilities as well. He was working at a time when children with learning disabilities were not thought to have an emotional life and very little study had been made of their emotional needs. Taking a developmental approach, I think it is possible to understand quite a lot about the early factors that can affect adult behaviour and I have never understood why childhood experiences are not given more weight in psychiatric practice. I hope that as President of the Royal College of Psychiatrists (2005–) I shall be able to influence the curriculum so that it has more of a developmental flavour.

Let me give you a few examples of current insights in the field of learning disability. We have a saying in my speciality, "If you can get it right for children and adults with learning disabilities, then you can probably get it right for everyone". Winnicott did mention that in providing residential homes for evacuated children who did not settle in their billets during the war, it was better to provide for those with mental defects separately. He said, "This is not only because they need special management and education, but also because they wear out the hostel staff to no purpose and cause a feeling of hopelessness." He wrote extensively about children with an antisocial tendency and failures in their early family experiences. My interest is in exploring what happens when this antisocial tendency, that he wrote so clearly about, persists in children who also have learning disabilities. I think there are some lessons that can be learned from my field and I want to show how my thinking has been influenced by Winnicott's teaching. However, without Brett Kahr's encouragement, I am not sure I would have felt I could have shared my experiences in the setting of this Memorial Lecture, so I turned first to his edited essays (Kahr, 2002) to remind me of some of Winnicott's influence in our field.

Winnicott said that, along with the dependency of early infancy, there is a period in which it is not possible to describe an infant without also describing the mother from whom the infant has not yet become able to be separate. That put me in mind of my first research project, which I did under Dr Brafman's supervision and presented at a Royal College meeting in the 1970s with the title "The sins of the fathers". This unpublished study looked at the case-notes of current children receiving therapy in the Roehampton Child Guidance Clinic and traced the records of their parents when they were children. We saw the same patterns of conduct and neurotic disorders in both generations, recognizing that there may, of course, be a genetic link as well as environmental and social links. Many of the parents, when still at primary school, had had conduct disorders and then gone on to be truants and delinquents in their teenage years. The question was, would this pattern repeat itself with their children—the children currently in the study—just as their earlier disturbances had mirrored their parents at a similar age? We did not follow those children but there are many studies showing continuity in children's behaviour patterns: for example, something recently written about boys' behaviour in the first year of life predicting the presence of attention-deficit hyperactivity disorders (ADHD) in primary school (Morrell & Murray, 2003); or Jane McCarthy's MD research, which I am supervising, which traces continuities in behaviour and psychiatric disorder in children with Down's Syndrome as they become adults.

In the learning disability field there is much written in Britain about so-called challenging behaviour; perhaps it could seen as an antisocial tendency. Challenging behaviour is called "challenging" because it is behaviour that challenges carers and service-providers, the idea being to put the locus outside the individual. One definition of challenging behaviour refers to behaviours of such an intensity, frequency, or duration, that the physical safety of the person, or of others, is likely to be placed in serious jeopardy (Emerson et al., 1987). Another one is behaviour that is likely seriously to limit or delay access to, and the use of, ordinary community facilities; I think that some of the behaviour that Rod Morgan spoke about could be described in such terms. Challenging behaviour is seen as having a communicative function and thus is a concept that should sit comfortably alongside psychoanalytic theories. However, when the concept is usually interpreted in practice, little attention is paid to developmental aspects of the child's or adult's personality.

I would like to introduce some other concepts, which I have developed in part with Dr Valerie Sinason, the psychoanalyst and child therapist who will be known to many of you, and with whom I have had the good fortune of working very closely for the past fifteen years. I called these aspects "the three secrets" (Hollins & Grimer, 1988); Valerie was simultaneously developing her "five mutative factors" (Sinason, 1992). I think these secrets, or factors, provide a link to Winnicott's writings and understanding. My secrets included the secrets of mortality, of sexuality, and of disability and dependency. Valerie's mutative factors added a fear of being annihilated, recognizing the hopeless and murderous feelings of some parents towards their disabled children. One of the secrets or factors is about continuing dependency, and this links to Winnicott's ideas about the way in which the infant needs to move from a completely dependent relationship with his mother to an increasingly independent one. I want to explore that a bit more—and I hope that people here who know much more about Winnicott's work than I do will forgive me if I rehearse a couple of his ideas here.

We are all familiar with the usual time-frame in which these developmental stages are worked through, and the way in which life's challenges can lead individuals to revert to more dependent ways of relating. It is much harder for children with learning disabilities to navigate these stages. Winnicott wrote about the effects of environmental failures on development and I am interested in the interaction and the combined effect of biological and environmental challenges. Let me give a few definitions, explain what I mean when I talk about learning disabilities. The Department of Health's White Paper, *Valuing People*, which was published in 2001, said that four per cent of children grow up with intellectual learning disabilities. Learning disability is defined as the presence of a "significantly reduced ability to understand new or complex information and learn new skills" (that is "impaired intelligence") with "a reduced ability to cope independently" (that is "impaired social functioning"), which "started before adulthood and has a lasting effect on development". It is not curable. One of the issues often raised by mental health workers who are not specialists in learning disability is that if something is not curable, is there anything you can do about it? Certainly, when I first started working in the psychiatry of learning disability, people would say that if you cannot cure their impairments, what is the point of working with such a child? I suppose the point really is that if you do accept that such children have emotional lives, then you can work with them and their emotional lives in the same way that you can work with anybody. The fact that you cannot cure the biological impairment does not mean that you cannot work with them at all—with their thinking, their feelings, and their ability to play. The majority of this population of four per cent will have quite a mild learning disability, and they may have no visible sign of difference, although the demography of learning disability is changing. There is recent evidence of an increased prevalence of learning disability, including many more children with severe learning disability because of improved neonatal survival. You may not know by looking at those with mild or moderate learning disabilities that there is anything different about them—but most will be functionally illiterate and innumerate and few will achieve the full independence that Winnicott describes.

Winnicott described three stages in the process of maturation (Winnicott, 1965), and I will briefly revisit them. In his first stage of absolute dependency of the infant, it is both the psychical and the physical environment that make possible steady progress towards maturation. Babies are unaware of the role that mother plays and of her essential care. This is so because the child, or the adult with a profound learning disability, has not yet made the distinction—and, in the case of the adult with the profound learning disability, may never make the distinction—between what is "Me" and what is "Not Me". At the second stage of relative dependence, when the child becomes aware of the dependent relationship with parents and begins to see himself or herself as a whole person, the distinction between me and not me has been made. Winnicott said that problems at this stage may lead to pathological states of dependency, or to defiance and violence. The child begins to make experiments towards independence but needs to be able to re-experience dependence. This stage lasts much longer in children with learning disabilities and many will not mature beyond this.

The third stage described is "working towards" independence. This stage is dependent upon the first two stages having been negotiated successfully. The child, through interaction with the external environment, has gradually been supported to meet the world in all its complexities. However, Winnicott reminds us that independence is never absolute and that the healthy individual is not isolated but relates to the environment in such a way that she or he and the environment are interdependent. Achieving that state remains particularly difficult in those with learning disabilities. The White Paper, *Valuing People*, identified some central principles for services and policy-makers to address, which include independence and inclusion. For many people these principles are necessarily going to be about supported independence—often described in terms of supported living, supported employment, and so on.

So what additional challenges do children with learning disabilities face? First of all, there are hundreds of genetic causes of learning disability; then there are some that are environmentally caused, including the effects of infection, or a head injury occurring in the developing child. It has been suggested that a lack of "good enough" mothering or care can in itself lead to learning disability. In most instances, however, there is a biological aetiology to the kind of learning disability that I am talking about.

Let's consider Foetal Alcohol Syndrome, as an exemplar. In the editorial of a recent *British Medical Journal* (Mukherjee & Hollins, 2005), with colleagues at St George's, we suggest that there may be no such thing as a safe drink in pregnancy, and we describe the devastating effect that alcohol can have on the developing brain. When the Foetal Alcohol Syndrome has been caused because the infant's mother has a serious and continuing alcohol addiction, then it is also possible that other environmental trauma and deprivation may further complicate the neurological damage that has been caused by the alcohol to the developing foetus. Our growing knowledge of the epidemiology of Foetal Alcohol Syndrome suggests that it may be the commonest cause of learning disability, and borderline learning disability, and that many young offenders may have some of the neuro-psychiatric deficits associated with it. These foetal alcohol effects are long-lasting and have devastating consequences for an individual's ability to, for example, negotiate and understand relationships. But these effects are still poorly understood. Educational and treatment programmes do not yet provide appropriate interventions. Many of the young people in the Youth Justice system are almost certainly the victims of alcohol abuse— from either the foetal alcohol effects themselves, or from some of the social and environmental influences of alcohol. One of the aims of our editorial in the *BMJ* is to raise awareness of the serious effects of alcohol on the health of some of the next generation; those children who will be the victims of our binge-drinking culture.

In her doctoral thesis, Valerie Sinason (University of London, 2004) postulated that the experience of being learning disabled, added to biological and environmental insults, together constituted a compound trauma. Many years ago she coined the term "secondary handicap" to describe failures of development experienced by people with learning disabilities, rather similar to the "false self" described by Winnicott, but emphasizing the additional deprivation that is contributory. Winnicott's idea was that true and false selves develop as a result of the quality of the mothering a child receives. The not-good-enough mother, who cannot understand and react to the child's non-verbal communications, expects the child to comply with her needs, rather than to adapt hers to the child's. Winnicott calls this compliance an expression of the false self and it is an important feature in Valerie's concept of secondary handicap, which she defines as a response that

> enables the individual to survive the societal response to the primary organic impairment. It is expressed by the way in which the organic problem is hidden or distorted by a defensive secondary process. . . . Secondary handicap takes many forms and often applies to walking, clothes, facial expressions, and speech. Whilst it has a protective functioning in defending against shame and trauma, it often outlives its usefulness and depletes the individual's relationship with those around him or her. [Sinason, 2004]

Through individual and group work with people with learning disabilities, it became apparent to Valerie that the process of stupefaction, a secondary handicapping process, was a defence against the trauma of disability and related abuse. Valerie and I run a clinic together every week where we see adults with learning disabilities who also have mental illness and/or challenging behaviour, many of whom have experienced abuse in their lives. We assess them for

individual and group psychotherapy and what has become particularly interesting is that during our assessment process the
secondary handicap is very quickly dropped once the people we
are seeing are able to understand that we are there to hear about
some of their pain. It is quite shocking for people who have not
worked with people with learning disabilities, either children or
adults, to see how quickly that defence can be dropped.

So what about crime? In another radio talk for parents, this time
in 1949 on "Stealing and telling lies", Winnicott commented that
". . . there is a very indistinct borderline between the common and
healthy stealing of the little child from his own mother, and the
thieving of the ill, older child." He went on to say that there is a
normal transition period in which the older child "begins to feel it
is wrong to steal things". For this transition to be made successfully,
parents are required to provide support and boundaries. We need
to recognize that for some children these boundaries are lacking. In
a quite remarkable piece of writing for teachers and care-workers
in 1947, Winnicott described further his work with evacuees during
the Second World War. It turned out that there was an extraordinarily large number of evacuated children who were having difficulty settling in their billets in the county where he was working as
a child psychiatrist. He wrote that one of his tasks was to protect
the public from the "nuisance" of some of these antisocial children,
and, as well as recognizing and responding to their "illness", he
had to recognize the unconscious public wish for revenge. Many of
the lessons he learned during those war years seem to me still to be
relevant to the needs of potential and actual young offenders today.
I particularly appreciated his description of the characteristics of a
good children's home and of a good warden, and his recognition
that psychotherapy was of no use without good-enough parenting
or substitute parenting. Talking to magistrates in 1946, he explained
his thoughts about the importance of understanding the unconscious and its relevance to their work as magistrates with juvenile
delinquents. He asked if some magistrates ". . . failed to see that
thieves are unconsciously looking for something more than bicycles
. . ." He also talked about their important role in dealing with this
unconscious public need for revenge and said it would be dangerous if magistrates adopted a "purely therapeutic aim". The child, he
said, in offending against society, is seeking to "re-establish control

from outside" and reminded them that "anti-social behaviour is at times no more than an SOS for control by strong, loving and confident people".

Let me mention briefly a study by researchers at Manchester University (Kroll et al., 2002); some of the statistics which Professor Morgan shared with us earlier are from a different, although similar, study. The research was designed to look at the mental health needs of boys in secure care and found that twenty-seven per cent of the ninety-seven offenders had an IQ below seventy; however, staggeringly, seventy per cent had an IQ below eighty-five. Now, it is expected that sixteen per cent of the whole population will have an IQ below eighty-five; so for seventy per cent of these young people to have an IQ below eighty-five is out of the ordinary. The researchers were looking at their mental health needs and the extent to which these needs had been assessed and/or met. They found that very little attention had been paid to even assessing their mental health, and this led to some important recommendations. Boys in secure care, they said, need better access to psychological treatment for emotional disorders; they have a high range of treatable problems, such as depression and anxiety. Second, they recommended better provision for assessment and treatment of aggressive behaviour—what in my field is called challenging behaviour. Finally, they identified a need for high quality programmes for substance misuse. The study concluded by emphasizing the importance of external factors in resolving or maintaining their difficulties, and stressed that intervention should not be restricted to secure units but must involve the family and the local communities to which the boys would eventually return.

Further evidence about the characteristics of young offenders with learning disabilities was provided by a study conducted for a higher degree in the University of London by my colleague Dr Ian Hall some years ago (Hall, 1997). He compared matched groups of young offenders with and without learning disabilities in secure care. He found that they had a similar frequency and type of psychiatric disorder, including suicidal thoughts—although suicidal acts seemed to be less common in those with learning disabilities. Those with learning disabilities had a high level of maladaptive behaviour, compared with those without learning disabilities and they were much more likely to have been cared for outside their family home. Their socialization and communication skills were more impaired, relative to their daily living skills and their IQ scores. I now wonder if some might have suffered from Foetal Alcohol Syndrome, or foetal alcohol effects?

What is the role of psychotherapy in all this? Some other research in my department at St George's is relevant to tonight's theme. We were asked to evaluate a new therapeutic initiative: an out-patient therapy group for young offenders, young abusers with learning disabilities (Nicholls, Hubert, Flynn, Sequeira, & Hollins, 2004). The six boys in the study ranged in age from thirteen to seventeen years. All were engaging in antisocial and sexually abusive behaviour; all of them had experienced multiple complex trauma, including early emotional deprivation and abuse in their own lives; all of them could be seen as having difficulties in negotiating Winnicott's stages of dependence "towards independence". The research team concluded that the boys showed some evidence of maturation after three years' experience of being in a group and only one of the boys reoffended during that period. But these teenagers continued to be highly vulnerable and to need high levels of well co-ordinated community support. That is not being adequately provided for them. One of the therapeutic controversies was whether the focus of the therapy should be on them as perpetrators or on them as victims. Interestingly enough, Valerie Sinason and I have found, in our work with adults whose behaviour was sexually inappropriate and abusive towards others, that until we focus on and work with them as victims, it really is not possible to be in touch with them as perpetrators. This approach seems to be considered as quite controversial in the learning disability field.

An ethnographic research project led by Jane Hubert (a social anthropologist also from St George's) described the experiences of men with severe learning disabilities living in a long-stay hospital (Hubert & Hollins, 2006). She writes that as young children, the sixteen men had lived at home with their families. When their behaviour became too difficult for their parents to manage, or for other family reasons, they were placed in children's hospitals on a long-term basis, later being transferred to the locked ward of an adult mental handicap hospital:

> When the men were admitted to hospital as young children, they were often described simply as "difficult to manage youngsters".

After many years of institutionalisation, they appeared to fulfil the popular stereotype of "mad people" in institutions. They flung themselves on to the floor, at the walls; they banged their heads; they roared and screeched; they tore their clothes; they injured each other or themselves. [Hubert & Hollins, 2006]

Jane spent more than 250 hours in the ward with these men, getting to know them. They were men with severe learning disabilities who were being prepared to move out of the hospital into the community; the idea was to try to get to know them a little, and to know their likes and dislikes, in preparation for the move. Most were, on the whole, non-verbal, but she does recount some stories where they did, on occasion, use speech. For example, one day she was talking to a man who usually tore his clothes and remained naked in that environment; she talked to him about how she had been to visit his father and told him what his father had said—his father had not visited for many years. This man stopped roaring and became very quiet; then he just said, "Bless you." She said she had never heard this man speak before; the nurses who were there had never heard him speak either.

Let me end with another quote, or an approximate one, from Winnicott:

So here we have the problem: children deprived of home life must be provided with something personal and stable when they are young enough to make use of it—or [they will] force us later to provide stability in an approved school or four walls in the shape of a prison cell. [Winnicott, 1968]

It is sixty years since Winnicott wrote that sentence. Little has changed. The same needs are there. Children with learning disabilities who have been similarly deprived have additional emotional needs and are crying out to be better understood and supported. Rod Morgan said nobody wants to help antisocial children. How much less, however, does anyone want to help children and young people with learning disabilities, who also have challenging behaviour or emotional mental health needs? I believe that antisocial young people, with or without learning disabilities, can be helped; can be better understood; and that we have an obligation to try and help them. Thank you.

References

Department of Health White Paper (2001). *Valuing People: A New Strategy for Learning Disability for the 21st Century*. London: Department of Health.

Emerson, E., Barrett, S., Bell, C., Cummings, R., McCool, C., Toogood, A., & Mansell, J. (1987). Developing services for people with severe learning disabilities and challenging behaviours. University of Kent at Canterbury, Institute of Social and Applied Psychology Report.

Hall, I. (1999). Young people with a learning disability with difficult or dangerous behaviour. MPhil thesis, Senate House, London.

Hollins, S. (1979). The sins of the fathers . . . the recurrence of family problems in the next generation, Abstract, Annual Meeting, The Royal College of Psychiatrists, Exeter, July.

Hollins S., & Grimer, M. (1988). *Going Somewhere: Pastoral Care for People with Learning Disability*. London: SPCK.

Hubert, J., & Hollins, S. (2006). Men with severe learning disabilities and challenging behaviour in long-stay NHS hospital care prior to discharge: a qualitative study. *British Journal of Psychiatry, 188*(1): 70–74.

Kahr, B. (Ed.) (2000). *Legacy of Winnicott Essays on Infant and Child Mental Health*. London: Karnac.

Kroll, L., Rothwell, J., Bradley, D., Shah, P., Bailey, S., & Harrington, R. C. (2002). Mental health needs of boys in secure care for serious or persistent offending: a prospective, longitudinal study. *The Lancet, 359*, 8 June, 1975–1979.

McCarthy, J. (2005). The mental health of young people with Down Syndrome: adult outcome and early risk. MD Thesis.

Morrell, J., & Murray, L. (2003). Parenting and the development of conduct disorder and hyperactive symptoms in childhood: a prospective longitudinal study from 2 months to 8 years. *Journal of Child Psychology & Psychiatry & Allied Disciplines, 44*(4): 489–508.

Mukherjee, R., & Hollins, S. (2005). Low level alcohol consumption and harm to the developing foetus; what level is safe? *British Medical Journal, 330*: 375–376.

Nicholls, L., Hubert, J., Flynn, M., Sequeira, H., & Hollins, S. (2004). Group psychodynamic therapy for sexual abusers: experiences and outcomes for adolescent boys with learning disabilities. Report to Hayward Foundation, St George's Hospital Medical School, London.

Sinason, V. (1992). *Mental Handicap and the Human Condition: New Approaches from the Tavistock.* London: Free Association Press.

Sinason, V. (2004). Learning disability as trauma and the impact of trauma on learning disability. PhD thesis, Senate House, London.

Smith, C., Algozzine, B., Schmid, R., & Hennly, T. (1990). Prison adjustment of youthful inmates with mental retardation. *Mental Retardation, 28*(3): 177–181.

Winnicott, D. W. (1947). Residential management as treatment for difficult children. In: J. Hardenburg (Ed.), *The Child and the Outside World: Studies in Developing Relationships.* London: Tavistock.

Winnicott, D. W. (1957)[1946]. What do we mean by a normal child? In: J. Hardenburg (Ed.), *The Child and the Family: First Relationships.* London: Tavistock.

Winnicott, D. W. (1965). *The Maturational Processes and the Facilitating Environment: Studies in the Theory of Emotional Development.* London: Hogarth.

Winnicott, D. W. (1968). Playing: its theoretical status in the clinical situation. *International Journal of Psychoanalysis, 49*(4): 591–599.

Envoi

Cesare Sacerdoti

Tonight's lecture reminded me of a Glover Memorial Lecture given by the former Inspector of HM Prisons, Sir David Ramsbotham, at the Tavistock & Portman Clinic a few years ago. Sir David, a military man with the pragmatic approach usually associated with discipline, in a short time demonstrated a deep sensibility and understanding of the environment in which he had to immerse himself. Although not primarily involved with young offenders, he found that psychotherapy within the prison service was of obvious and essential importance if one was to hope for rehabilitation and, above all, to avoid—or at least contain—the perpetuation of crime from one generation to the following one.

Here, tonight, we have had the privilege of listening to Rod Morgan, an eminent academic in the legal field, whose concern is solely with children and young offenders. Many of us would perhaps tend to associate somebody in that field with punishment above all; instead, we have heard a compassionate and realistic approach to the problem and it has been particularly touching to hear what happens to such children—the harsh truths about what can happen and, unfortunately, how comparatively little is being done to help them. By justice, Rod Morgan does not mean retribution and vengeance, but professionalism informed by compassion. The problem of children who offend does not concern only the Youth Justice Board, although most in society would prefer that it was; would prefer not to think about it; would prefer to hide it away and forget all about it. But society has to take responsibility for the problem and supply the means to deal with it to those professionals who not only care, but also have the ability to devise ways that may either prevent it arising in the first place, or to rehabilitate offenders.

Sheila Hollins' talk also showed that compassion is the main ingredient that has enabled her to understand and deal effectively with mental health problems, particularly those of children, which can have such deleterious effects on both the individuals and society. Her odyssey to understanding and action was also prompted and guided by her innate empathy, allied to trained professionalism. The fact that she continues to seek additional training and broader experience in her chosen field, tells us again how much she cares for these young people.

Our thanks to you both, Sheila and Rod, not only from all of us here tonight but also, I would dare to say, on behalf of the young people whom you both care about and help in your professional lives.

Appendix

Winnicott's contribution to the study of dangerousness

Brett Kahr

Since the inauguration of the International Association for Forensic Psychotherapy in 1991, and the creation of the world's first diploma course in forensic psychotherapy in 1994 under the joint auspices of the British Postgraduate Medical Federation of the University of London, and the Portman Clinic, the psychoanalytic study and treatment of both perverse and delinquent patients has become an increasingly visible and important area of expertise within the mental health field. Spurred on by the foundational work of Dr Estela Welldon, who first coined the term "forensic psychotherapy", this arena of study has become increasingly visible in recent years, and now, for the first time, the Royal College of Psychiatrists of the United Kingdom has created a specialist training in forensic psychotherapy for psychiatric registrars. After a long and continuous struggle, it has become much more possible for workers to offer psychological treatment to the offender-patient, rather than the proverbial punishment.

Although many of us derive great pleasure from the innovativeness and freshness of the newly constituted profession of forensic psychotherapy, we must not forget that the roots of psychoanalytic work with dangerous and perverse individuals reach back at least into the very early years of the last century. Sigmund Freud, the founder of psychoanalysis, would have had the opportunity to observe many violent and uncontained patients in the Allgemeines Krankenhaus on the outskirts of Vienna; and though Freud did not focus on forensic patients as such, he did treat at least one paedophile patient (Kahr, 1999), and he provided supervision for a paedophile patient under the care of his student Theodor Reik (Kahr, 1991; Natterson, 1966). Sigmund Freud maintained an extremely sympathetic attitude to forensic matters, and in his letter to the convicted felon Georg Fuchs, Freud lamented the horrific punishments meted out to prisoners, which Freud himself regarded as "a manifestation of the brutality and the folly that dominate present civilized mankind" (quoted in Eissler, 1961, p. 199).

Freud also wrote an important essay on psychoanalysis and criminology, entitled "Psycho-Analysis and the Establishment of the Facts in Legal Proceedings" (1906b), as well as an article on "Some Character-Types Met with in Psycho-Analytic Work" (1916d), which contains the memorable section entitled "Criminals from a Sense of Guilt", in which he first espoused the notion that criminality begins in the phantasy life of the patient and that unconscious ideas lurk at the base of deviant behaviour. By under-scoring the notion that delinquency stems from motivational causes, Freud provided us with the bedrock of subsequent theories in forensic psychotherapy. Sadly, Freud himself missed out on what may well have proved to be the most exciting piece of forensic consultation work. In 1924, he received an invitation to serve as a well-remunerated expert witness in the highly publicized American murder case in which two young men from Chicago, Nathan Leopold and Richard Loeb, stood trial for a brutal slaying. For reasons that remain not entirely clear to biographers, Freud refused to cooperate in the trial, despite the offer of a fee of $25,000 (Jones, 1957).

Other important works by Freud on forensically related matters include his little-known essay on "The Acquisition and Control of Fire" (1932a), which provides material on the psychogenesis of arson and pyromania. Freud also wrote insightfully about male homosexuality (1910c, 1911c [1910]), and female homosexuality (1920a), beating experiences (1919e), fetishism (1927e), parricide (1928b), and many other topics besides (cf. 1925f, 1931d).

Donald Winnicott has provided us with an extremely useful assessment of Freud's contribution to the study of forensic topics. In his classic essay "Psycho-Analysis and the Sense of Guilt", delivered in honour of Freud's centenary, Winnicott (1958a) wrote that, "More than anyone else it was Freud who paved the way for the understanding of antisocial behaviour and of crime as a sequel to an unconscious criminal intention, and a symptom of a failure in child-care" (pp. 31–32). Indeed, Winnicott's crisp summary aptly highlights the major ideas espoused by Freud—namely, that crime and perversion begin in the nursery.

Winnicott derived great inspiration from the work of Freud, and he even dedicated his book on children's medicine to Professor Freud (Winnicott, 1931) in gratitude. In the pages that follow, I shall undertake an examination of the ideas of Dr Donald Woods Winnicott (1896–1971), one of the most prolific and seminal pioneers of forensic psychotherapy, whose contribution to the field of delinquency remains of lasting value for practitioners of mental health.

Born in Plymouth in the county of Devon on 7 April 1896, Winnicott will undoubtedly be best remembered for his incomparable work in the field of infant mental health and child psychotherapy (Kahr, 1996a,b, 2000, 2002). But Winnicott also wrote extensively and prolifically about a variety of forensic subjects, and it seems only fitting to pay tribute to this work. After a lengthy formation in the natural sciences at Jesus College of the University of Cambridge, followed by medical studies at St. Bartholomew's Hospital in London, Winnicott became a specialist in children's medicine. By 1924, he realized that he would have to undergo psychoanalytic training if he wished to provide comprehensive medico-psychological treatment for his many child patients at the Paddington Green Children's Hospital. After consulting with Dr Ernest Jones, the president of the British Psycho-Analytical Society, Winnicott embarked on a ten-year personal analysis with James Strachey, a Bloomsbury habitué who had only recently returned from an analysis with Freud in Vienna.

By 1934, Winnicott had qualified as a psychoanalyst of adult patients, and in 1935 he received his certification as a psychoanalyst of children. Even by this relatively early date in his career, Winnicott had already started to work with violent patients. More than twenty years later, Winnicott (1956b) would recall his first child training patient thus:

> For my first child analysis I chose a delinquent. This boy attended regularly for a year and the treatment stopped because of the disturbance that the boy caused in the clinic. I could say that the analysis was going well, and its cessation caused distress both to the boy and to myself in spite of the fact that on several occasions I got badly bitten on the buttocks. The boy got out on the roof and also he spilt so much water that the basement became flooded. He broke into my locked car and drove it away in bottom gear on the self-starter. The clinic ordered termination of the treatment for the sake of the other patients. He went to an approved school. [p. 306]

He continued to develop his forensic work in a variety of settings, most particularly during the Second World War, when he served as a consultant psychiatrist to the Government Evacuation Scheme, advising staff members of residential hostels, strewn throughout the Oxfordshire countryside, about the management of severely psychotic and delinquent children, many of whom had lost one or both parents during the Blitz on London. All in all, Winnicott maintained psychiatric responsibility for some 285 children, who made quite a nuisance of themselves by terrorizing the local townspeople, setting fire to hayricks, running away, and so forth (Winnicott & Britton, 1944, 1947). The staff became easily demoralized from caring for such abused and abusing children, most of whom suffered from the "double traumatization" of having already come from difficult backgrounds and then succumbed to the terrors of war. Winnicott provided indispensable supervision. According to Clare Winnicott (1984), formerly Clare Britton, the psychiatric social worker in charge of the hostels,

> These sessions with him were the highlight of the week and were invaluable learning experiences for us all including Winnicott, who kept careful records of each child's situation and the stresses put on staff members. His comments were nearly always in the form of questions which widened the discussion and never violated the vulnerability of individual members. [p. 3]

According to contemporary psychoanalytic terminology, I suppose that we could describe Winnicott as a man who possessed a very finely developed "digestive capacity"—in other words, the ability to tolerate potent affects that other people might ignore or defend against. For instance, on 3 March 1943, Dr Elizabeth Rosenberg, a psychiatrist and psychoanalyst, presented a paper to an evening meeting of the British Psycho-Analytical Society on the war neuroses (Rosenberg, 1943). During the talk, an air-raid siren began to blare quite loudly, but the psychoanalysts seemed to pay no attention to the potential external danger. According to Dr Margaret Little, an eyewitness on that particular occasion, Winnicott rose to his feet, and called out, "I should like to point out that there is an air-raid going on" (quoted in Little, 1985, p. 19). He then suggested that the assembled company ought to walk downstairs to the air-raid shelter, but nobody responded to Winnicott's suggestion, and Dr Rosenberg continued to deliver her paper. As a source of inspiration to all good forensic practitioners, Winnicott proved able to tolerate the painful, external reality of the Blitz and to recommend appropriate managerial action.

Winnicott developed his psychoanalytic practice throughout the 1940s and 1950s, and he soon became one of the most respected psychoanalytic clinicians and thinkers in the country, renowned for his capacity to work with unbearable patients. In the course of writing a biography of Winnicott (Kahr, 1996a), I had the opportunity to meet many of Winnicott's former analytical patients; it soon became quite apparent that the vast majority had had previous, unsatisfactory experiences of psychotherapy or psychoanalysis with other practitioners, most of whom seemed incapable of helping the more distressed patient. In the tradition of many good forensic workers, Winnicott possessed the capacity to be simultaneously concerned as well as unfazed or unfrightened by his more disturbed and vulnerable patients, and his reputation for dealing with those who could not find help elsewhere soon grew and grew. Winnicott eventually rose to the rank of president of the British Psycho-Analytical Society, serving two terms, first from 1956 until 1959, and then again from 1965 until 1968. He died at his home in Belgravia, in southwest London, on 25 January 1971 at the age of 74.

Although Winnicott never worked in a traditional forensic setting, such as a prison or a medium-secure unit, he sustained a lively interest in forensic topics throughout his long clinical career. Not only did he work extensively with antisocial children and adolescents (Kahr, 1996b; Winnicott, 1956b), but he worked closely with the legal profession and with the probation service as well. For example, in 1967, he spoke to the Borstal Assistant Governors' Conference at King Alfred's College in Winchester, delivering his peerless paper on "Delinquency as a Sign of Hope" (1968), which eventually appeared in the Prison Service Journal, read by many probation officers.

A mere glance at the published volume of his selected correspondence (Winnicott, 1987) reveals ample evidence of Winnicott's continuous interest in forensic issues and concerns. In an intelligent letter, written to the Editor of The Times, Winnicott (1949b) pontificated about juvenile crime and about the management of Holloway Gaol, referring to the "knotty problem of crime and insanity". He further reflected that, "It is very seldom that the comments of a psychoanalyst are asked for or printed; instead it is assumed that the psychologist has an attitude, probably a sentimental one. The idea that psychoanalysis has no attitude, but that it can enlighten, seldom percolates" (p. 15). Through his frequent letters to politicians, ministers, and newspapers, Winnicott worked hard in his spare time in an attempt to enlighten public attitudes towards crime, emphasizing that psychoanalysis might make a very important contribution to the debate around working with highly distressed individuals. In that same letter, Winnicott (1949b) reminded his reader that we must not only consider the origins of crime, but also the fact that "there is another half of every antisocial act to be considered—society's revenge feelings" (p. 16), suggesting that much punishment stems from unconscious revenge on the part of the rest of us who have not committed overt criminal acts.

On 1 September 1949, Winnicott addressed two separate letters to government ministers, arguing to R. S. Hazlehurst that, "Stealing has practically no more relation to poverty and want than civil murder has to persecution" (Winnicott, 1949c, p. 17), and to S. H. Hodge that criminals actually suffer from psychological problems (Winnicott, 1949d), both of which were pioneering concepts in Great Britain in the immediate postwar period. Amid the zeal of punishing those who perpetrate crimes, Winnicott represented a voice of particular humanity, urging that both psychiatric patients and criminals alike deserve the right to successful psychotherapeutic treatment.

Winnicott discovered a simultaneously gentle and firm means of becoming an agitator for the field of forensic psychopathology. In his communication to Dr P. D. Scott, a well-known consultant psychiatrist at the Maudsley Hospital, Winnicott (1950b) reflected that,

> There is no doubt whatever that even if our knowledge of the psychopathology of criminology were to be complete tomorrow, there would still be a very great number of years before psychotherapists could be properly trained in numbers sufficient to make a practical difference to the problem. [p. 23]

But he remained optimistic that such work could be undertaken, and he even chided his mentor, Melanie Klein, and their colleagues within the British Psycho-Analytical Society for having neglected to study the psychology of delinquency in sufficient detail (Winnicott, 1952; cf. Winnicott, 1948b, 1953b).

Above all, Winnicott drew upon his unique wealth of clinical experience to alert us to the fact that delinquency results from deprivation in early infancy and childhood. We have yet to grapple with the implications of this important concept, outlined most clearly in his pivotal essay "The Antisocial Tendency" (Winnicott, 1956b; cf. Winnicott, 1943, 1945, 1948a, 1949a, 1956b, 1960a, 1961b, 1963c). Beginning with the case of a young boy called "John", a lad who engaged in compulsive stealing from shops, Winnicott traced a theory in which he hypothesized that stealing represents not only an aggressive act towards the object, but also something rather hopeful, an indication that the child realizes that something has gone missing—usually parental love—and that the act of theft can serve as a means of attempting to compensate for early, lost psychic nutrients. Cleverly, Winnicott described how he had enlisted the cooperation of John's mother so that she could better understand the roots of her young son's offending behaviour. Winnicott explained to John's mother:

> "Why not tell him that you know that when he steals he is not wanting the things that he steals but he is looking for something that he has a right to: that he is making a claim on his mother and father because he feels deprived of their love." I told her to use language which he could understand. [Winnicott, 1956b, p. 307]

John's mother absorbed Winnicott's thinking on this matter, and she attempted to discuss the problem with her son. She wrote to Winnicott some time later:

> "I told him that what he really wanted when he stole money and food and things was his mum; and I must say I didn't really expect him to understand, but he did seem to. I asked him if he thought we didn't love him because he was so naughty sometimes, and he said right out that he didn't think we did, much. Poor little scrap! I felt so awful, I can't tell you." [quoted in Winnicott, 1956b, p. 307]

But Winnicott always encouraged patients to engage in verbalization rather than enactment. Indeed, when Richard Balbernie, a colleague from the child mental health field, wrote to Winnicott enquiring whether foul language should be tolerated in children, Winnicott (1969b) replied, "How much nicer is hate than murder and how silly we are if we mind when children scream out 'fuck' and other obscenities" (cf. Kahr, 1998).

Winnicott established an overt aetiological link between deprivation and delinquency, and he expressed the view that if we manage to intervene early in childhood situations, then the prognosis will be very good indeed. However, mindful of the fact that many cases of seemingly intractable criminality and psychopathology do present themselves in adulthood, workers often become depressed and despondent, particularly when confronted with deeply entrenched behaviour. For this very reason, Winnicott wrote his remarkable paper "Delinquency as a Sign of Hope" (1968), encouraging workers to respond with reliability to delinquents, to help provide for something that could not be offered in the early, maturational years.

Winnicott's contributions to the field of forensic psychotherapy and to the study of severe psychopathology deserve a book-length treatment, and a lifetime's study. One will be very hard-pressed indeed to summarize the essence of Winnicott's fifty years as a health care professional, from the time of his qualification as a medical doctor in 1920 until his death in 1971. It remains my hope that students will find themselves drawn to read Winnicott's texts for the first time, and that experienced practitioners will return to Winnicott's publications, as sources of inspiration and elucidation, and above all, compassion, for the deeply turbulent patients who often enter our consulting-rooms.

* * *

Before he died, Winnicott began to work on an autobiography, which he never managed to complete, entitled *Not Less Than Everything*. On the very opening page, Winnicott inscribed the following plea: "Oh God! May I be alive when I die" (quoted in C. Winnicott, 1978, p. 19). Although Winnicott could not survive his own mortality, his ideas continue to remain as vibrant as ever, and they provide us with many areas of assistance in the ongoing task of trying to treat and rehabilitate those suffering from psychosis or personality disorders. I trust that *Forensic Psychotherapy and Psychopathology: Winnicottian Perspectives* will serve as a source of clinical sustenance to those of us who have committed ourselves to this continuously challenging field of clinical endeavour.